ONE-A-DAY'S FOR LEADERS

THOUGHTS AND QUOTES FOR
SUCCESSFUL LEADERSHIP

IN THE BEGINNING

My first management appointment
came after working several years in
support positions. I.B.M. Corporation
located in Boca Raton, Florida was my
employer from 1968 to 1989.

Knowing how important appreciation was
to me, my immediate approach in
communicating with subordinates, peers
and upper level management was
positive and upbeat.

I determined I would, every day, deliberately
compliment each person with whom I
came into contact.

I would regularly solicit their ideas and input
as to how to optimize our work efforts and
space. Even if we were doing well, I would
ask how we could do even better.
How could we be more efficient and effective?

COOPERATION & TEAMWORK

Cooperation and teamwork from that first
day forward, created outstanding results
in our first year together.

Utilizing my employees suggestions and
ideas, we made positive changes
and improvements to our department's
work assignments.

I promoted two of the twelve people in
our department and reduced overtime from
25 percent to 10 percent without replacing
them. PRODUCTIVITY...

After requesting less money in the budget
than the previous manager had in his
budget, our group efforts resulted
in a positive balance of$260,000.00
at the end of the first year.

This netted a promotion for me after my
first year in management...all because of the
people working for me. They responded
to a totally positive working environment.

One of my first year employees gave me
a book, The One Minute Manager. He
said "You need to read this...it's about
you".

USE YOUR IMAGINATION AND CREATE A POSITVE ENVIRONMENT.

Just as one-a-day vitamins are good for the body, One-A-Day compliments and comments are good for positive morale and production.

With some imagination, you can develop ways to establish a totally positive work atmosphere.

Daily compliments, positive comments can be a simple as...

telling someone how nicely they are dressed.

How about "I really like how you.... or maybe " you do such a good job and I appreciate your consistency"

There are so many ways you can compliment or comment positively.

<u>With deliberate, regular practice, it will become a natural habit.</u>

SOME ATTRIBUTES OF
AN EFFECTIVE LEADER

Presents a positive attitude when times
are good and when times are bad.

Shows appreciation and praises efforts
regularly. I suggest daily...

Regularly solicits idea and suggestions
from all levels, especially subordinates.
Will evaluate quickly and implement
wherever possible.

Keeps personal information confidential.

Always shows respect for all individuals.

Keeps everyone informed of current
status of the business and organization.

Knows his/her successes are directly
related to the combined efforts
of everyone.

**YOU DO NOT HAVE TO HAVE
A FANCY TITLE TO BE A LEADER.**

When you work hard, with integrity,
giving your best efforts, others
notice and willing follow your example.

You can be an assembly worker,
a secretary, even a custodian
and still be a leader.

AN EFFECTIVE LEADER

<u>Listens as closely to subordinates</u> as he/she does to peers and superiors and always attempts to find merit in their suggestions.

<u>Works aggressively to resolve and remove obstacles</u> which prevent subordinates from giving their best performances.

Provides the best accomodations/tools possible to allow optimum performance.

Fully understands the meaning...
People don't' care how much you know until they know how much you care.

NOTE:

In a combined work effort, one where several processes are needed to complete a task, treat everyone involved as though they are your customers, give them what they need when they need it and you all succeed.

INTIMIDATION

So much research has been done and so many books written which prove the best results in any organization come from establishing and maintaining a positive environment.

Why, then, do so many people in leadership positions still attempt to utilize intimidation as a means of motivation?

IT DOES NOT WORK!

<u>*Praise, recognition and appreciation will be alive long after intimidation dies.*</u>

Intimidation works for a very short while... usually about as long as the boss is standing and watching. Let the boss get out of site and watch the employee deliberately slow down the work pace.

"Did I mention...a positive environment gets the best efforts and best production results?"

SOME THINGS GOOD
LEADERS NEVER DO...

...That is unless you wish to be one of life's
real jerks and relationships and success
mean nothing to you.

GOOD LEADERS NEVER...

Use profanity, especially when it is
directed at others. It degrades people
and tends to kill any chance of
cooperation and performance.

The use of profanity leaves the appearance
you are not intelligent enough to think of
the proper way to express yourself.

GOOD LEADERS NEVER...

Yell at subordinates, superiors or peers.
This is a definite sign you are unprofessional
and out of control.

AS A GOOD LEADER...

You can not be positive one day and negative the next. Inconsistency is a sure way to lose respect and cooperation.

Being an effective leader takes every day effort.

WORK ETHIC...

A good leader's work ethic is
key to guiding those who follow...

*Always work as though pride
and integrity are watching you.*

TRUST YOUR SUBORDINATES...

*The way to get your subordinates
to trust you is to trust them first.*

TRUST EMPLOYEES' KNOWLEDGE AND ABILITIES...

When one knows his or her job responsibilities and carries them out well, leave them alone let them perform.

NEVER TRY TO CHANGE THE HAT OF A PERSON WHO ALREADY HAS ONE THAT FITS.

WORK RELATIONSHIPS ARE TWO-WAY STREETS

The best way to keep a leader happy
is to produce. Likewise,
the best way to keep subordinates
happy is to express sincere appreciation
when they produce.

CHANGE IS GOOD WHEN PROPERLY MANAGED...

Make changes gradually. Too much too fast will cost you in morale and profits. Too many changes too fast, create confusion as well as loss in production.

DON'T BITE OFF MORE THAN YOU CAN CHEW...

Small changes can produce small problems...easy to correct.

Large changes can produce large problems...much harder and more costly to correct.

BE CAREFUL OF YOUR
JUDEMENT OF OTHERS...

Be sure you know all facts when drawing
conclusions. Wrong judgments result in
long-term negative affects on business
organizations as well as individuals.
One wrong judgment can't destroy
morale.

*Benefit of the doubt is a key to
healthy relationships.*

NEGATIVE COMMENTS
AND ACTIONS...

A wise leader will spend much of his/her
time expressing positive comments to
and around subordinates, peers and
superiors.

Negative comments will always breed
negative results.

Negative leaders will hide in the shadows
In attempt to catch someone doing
something wrong.

Let me suggest....

*Try sneaking upon someone with the
intention of catching them doing
something right.
You just might succeed.*

SUCCESSFUL LEADERS
LEAD BY EXAMPLE

Set positive tones for your organization
by your words and actions.

*The more positive the environment,
the more positive the work results.*

You set the tone.

RESPECT ALL INDIVIDUALS

Good leaders never talk negatively about one subordinate to another.

They don't "run down" the bosses or company to employees.

Good leaders undergird superiors as well as peers and subordinates.

**A CONFIDENT LEADER NEVER
HAS TO TRY AND PROVE
HE OR SHE IS THE BOSS**

*Job titles are only good for scope of
responsibility. Otherwise, people
are people and willingly follow those
qualified, positive leaders.*

WANT SUBORDINATES TO "BUY-IN" TO WHAT YOU WISH TO ACCOMPLISH?

A wise leader will not waste time trying to prove how much he/she knows…likewise will spend a great deal of time listening and learning how much the subordinate knows, then capitalize by utilizing those ideas and suggestions.

CONFIDENCE AND RESPECT

People, when treated with confidence and respect, more often than not, will provide positive work results.

LEADERS HEAR EXCUSES AT TIMES AND IT IS EASY TO OVERLOOK THE REASONS THINGS HAPPEN

Eliminate the reasons things happen to cause production losses, then it is quite easy to expose the excuses for lack of results.

THERE IS NOTHING WRONG WITH BEING NICE. KIND, POSITIVE WORDS AND ACTIONS BUILD MOUNTAINS OF GOOD WILL.

Negative words and actions create the lowest of valleys which allow floods of destruction.

EXPERIENCE

Thirty plus years of leading utilizing positive, encouraging techniques, convinced me the information you have found in this book work.

BASIC BEHAVIOR

It begins at an early age.

The more you praise a child, the less discipline is necessary.

Adults, like children, respond positively and appropriately to praise and recognition.

<u>I now challenge you to adopt this One-A-Day approach. My experience has convinced me it works.</u>